The Negro as a Soldier in the war of the Rebellion

REBECCA.

A SLAVE GIRL FROM NEW ORLEANS

THE

NEGRO AS A SOLDIER

IN THE

WAR OF THE REBELLION.

BY

NORWOOD P. HALLOWELL,

COLONEL, FIFTY-FIFTH REGIMENT, MASSACHUSETTS VOLUNTEERS.

READ BEFORE THE MILITARY HISTORICAL SOCIETY OF
MASSACHUSETTS, JANUARY 5, 1892.

BOSTON:
LITTLE, BROWN, AND COMPANY.
1897.

University Press:

JOHN WILSON AND SON, CAMBRIDGE, U.S.A.

THE NEGRO AS A SOLDIER

IN THE

WAR OF THE REBELLION.

————◆————

ONCE upon a time, at our old home in Philadelphia, there were two little girls whose names were Rebecca and Rosa. They had Caucasian features, an abundance of long wavy hair, and complexions that were suggestive merely of a clime sunnier than our own. Taking one of their hands into your own, your eye might have discovered at the finger tips a color of a darker hue than the other parts. It was the fatal single drop of negro blood that cursed the whole beautiful fabric and made it possible for these children to be fugitive slaves. Hid away in the barn of our country residence was another fugitive, — a tall, lithe, muscular man, black as anthracite, Daniel Dangerfield by name, now forgotten no doubt, but then enjoying for a brief period a national reputation. The police force of Philadelphia was watching for that man. The detectives looked mysterious as they went about on their false scents and failed to see our Daniel as he passed on to the next station of the Underground Railroad, comfortably seated in my mother's carriage, the curtains drawn, my brother Edward on the box quite ready to use

1

his five-shooter, and a younger brother in the less heroic
part of driver.

These fugitive-slave scenes, once so familiar, are recalled
because, to appreciate correctly the military significance of
the arming of citizens of African descent, it is necessary to
forget for the moment the great "Amendments," and to
remember the old times. To estimate the colored man
as a soldier it is essential to recall his status before the
war, for the reason that his previous condition of slavery
in the South, and his social, political, commercial and
religious ostracism in the North, ought naturally, and in
fact does do somewhat, to interpret his qualities when
bearing arms. The subject is complex The characteristics of the English are such that the expression, an
"English soldier," conveys a distinct idea; the words, a
"German soldier," at once suggest a well-defined picture.
To say simply a "French soldier" gives still another well-
understood type. A "negro soldier" or "colored soldier"
conveys, no doubt, to most minds some similar plain
meaning; but is the impression made necessarily a correct
one? Is not the expression "a colored soldier" as vague
as the expression "a white soldier"? I think it is. Had
we only to deal with the thick-lipped negro of Congo, the
subject would be simple enough. But we are dealing
now with the soldiers of a people in whose veins is an
admixture of the blood of every nationality that is repre-
sented on this continent. The blood that coursed through
the veins of our little slave girls was, barring the one
fatal drop, the same blood that coursed through the veins
of one of the proud families of Louisiana, — a family that
sent its sons, the white ones, to our New England col-
leges. It was not the same thing — ninety-nine one hun-

dredths of it was not — that flowed beneath the skin of Daniel Dangerfield, innocent as he was, apparently, of any such admixture, and yet it is all called "negro."

Nicholas Said, a private in our Fifty-fifth Massachusetts Regiment, was a native of Bornou, Eastern Soudan, Central Africa. He was tattooed on his forehead after the manner of the ruling class of his tribe. His linguistic ability was very marked. In the regiment he wrote and spoke fluently the English, French, German and Italian languages; while there is no doubt that he was master of Kanouri, (his vernacular), Mandra, Arabic, Turkish and Russian, — a total of nine languages. The First Louisiana Native Guards, mustered into the service at New Orleans, were recruited from the free colored population of that city. They are described as men of "property and education, a self-reliant and intelligent class." "The darkest of them," said General Butler, "were about the complexion of the late Mr. Webster." [1] On the other hand, the First South Carolina Regiment had not one mulatto in ten, and all the enlisted men had been slaves.

Such, in part, were the heterogeneous materials that made up our colored regiments. Obviously, it will not be safe to draw many arbitrary conclusions and to brand the whole as distinctively African. Avoiding, however, any further consideration of the difficulties suggested by ethnology, let us interpret the colored soldier as best we may by a partial review of his record in the War of the Slaveholders' Rebellion. "The war for the Union was not the first one in which the African fought for the liberties of our country. Black faces were not uncommon among the ranks of the patriots in Seventeen hundred

[1] Higginson's History of Black Regiments, 1.

Seventy-six. The first man to fall in that struggle was Crispus Attucks, who led the mob in its attack on the British troops at the Boston Massacre. At Bunker Hill the free negroes fought intermingled with the whites; and when Major Pitcairn was killed, it was by a bullet from a negro's rifle. At the battle of Rhode Island, Colonel Greene's black regiment repulsed three successive charges, during which they handled a Hessian regiment severely. In the War of 1812 General Jackson issued a proclamation authorizing the formation of black regiments, and subsequently, in an address to the colored troops thus enlisted, acknowledged their services in unstinted praise." [1] General Washington, with characteristic caution, wrote to Henry Laurens: "The policy of our arming slaves is in my opinion a moot point, unless the enemy set the example. . . . Besides, I am not clear that a discrimination will not render slavery more irksome to those who remain in it." He adds, however, that these are "only the first crude ideas" that struck him. Alexander Hamilton, on the other hand, gave his unqualified and hearty support to the measure. "An essential part of the plan," he urged, "is to give them their freedom with their muskets." [2]

The first systematic attempt to recruit colored men in the War of the Rebellion was made by General Hunter at Hilton Head. His effort was valuable as an example of how not to do it. Impatient at the slow progress of his work, he made the fatal mistake of forcing the freedmen into the ranks. While working on the plantations they were rudely seized by squads of soldiers and taken into

[1] Fox's Regimental Losses, 52.
[2] Livermore's Historical Research, 163.

camp as prisoners. Here they were told by their enemies that they were to be returned to slavery or sent to Cuba There was no mutual confidence between officers and men. Desertions were numerous, discontent general. In five months the regiment was disbanded without pay. One company, however, maintained its organization, doing some good work by hunting down and driving the rebels from St. Simon's Island, — a job that had been initiated by the colored residents of the island themselves. Twenty-five of these natives had armed themselves, under the command of one of their own number, whose name was John Brown. He was ambuscaded and shot dead, probably the first black man, says Colonel T. W. Higginson, whose recital I am following, almost literally, who fell under arms in the war. This was the first armed encounter, so far as known, between the rebels and their former slaves; and it is worth noticing that the attempt was a spontaneous thing, and not accompanied by any white man. The men were not soldiers, nor in uniform. The rebel leader, one Miles Hazard, and his party made good their escape. In the following year there was captured at the railroad station in Jacksonville, Florida, a box of papers. Among them was a letter from this very Hazard to a friend describing the perils of that adventure, and saying, "If you wish to know hell before your time, go to St. Simon's and be hunted ten days by niggers."[1]

The arming of slaves by Major-General Hunter, and a similar movement initiated by Brigadier-General Phelps at New Orleans, stirred President Jefferson Davis to the innermost recesses of his unhappy mind. On August 20th, 1862, he directed that both generals should be no

[1] Higginson's History of Black Regiments, 275.

longer held and treated as public enemies of the Confederate States, but as outlaws ; and that in the event of the capture of either of them, or that of any other commissioned officer employed in drilling, organizing or instructing *slaves*, with a view to their armed service in the war, he should not be regarded as a prisoner of war, but held in close confinement for execution as a felon at such time and place as might be ordered.   On May 1, 1863, the Confederate Congress passed an act which outlawed all commissioned white officers who should command negroes or mulattoes, *whether slaves* or *free*, in arms against the Confederate States.

The attention of the country at large was first seriously directed to the consideration of this new element in the army when Governor John A. Andrew obtained an order from Edwin M. Stanton, Secretary of War, authorizing him to organize persons of African descent into separate corps for the volunteer military service.   As a consequence, a line of recruiting depots, running from Boston to St. Louis in the West, and to Fortress Monroe in the South, was established and maintained to the close of the war. Two infantry regiments, the Fifty-fourth and Fifty-fifth, and one cavalry, the Fifth, were raised, and the ranks kept at the maximum number; a good piece of work, involving an immense amount of labor, which was done mainly by two citizens of Medford, — George L. Stearns and Richard P. Hallowell.

Public opinion in the North was either avowedly hostile to this scheme or entirely sceptical as to its value.   In Philadelphia, recruiting was attended with some little danger, and with so much annoyance that the place of rendezvous was kept secret and the squads were marched under cover of darkness to the depot. In Ohio it was considered a good joke to get the "darkies on to Massachusetts,"—a joke that was bitterly repented when Ohio at a later day tried in vain to get those same "darkies" credited to her quota. In Boston there were contemptuous remarks by individuals from both extremes of society; by certain members of a prominent club, who later on hissed the Fifty-fourth Regiment from their windows as it marched on its way to the front; and by a Boston journal whose editors disgraced their columns with reflections too vulgar for repetition. There was, too, much good-natured laughing and harmless joking among other classes. Before long, however, the prevailing undertone of thought became thoroughly respectful and kind, while the pecuniary aid given was limited only by the amount asked for.

The colored man from the free States as a soldier may be conveniently and fairly tested by the record of our Massachusetts regiments, for the reason, as we shall see later, that those regiments contained every known variety of citizen of African descent, and were recruited from every class and condition of colored society. That the Massachusetts regiments were not composed of picked men, except as to physique, is conclusively shown by the statistics. Those of the Fifty-fifth are here given. Those of the Fifty-fourth do not materially differ.

STATISTICS OF THE FIFTY–FIFTH REGT. MASS. VOLS.

BIRTHPLACE.

Maine	1	New Jersey	8
Vermont	1	Pennsylvania	139
Massachusetts	22	Maryland	19
Rhode Island	3	Virginia	106
Connecticut	4	North Carolina	30
New York	23	Georgia	6

Alabama	5	Tennessee		24
Mississippi	9	Michigan		8
Louisiana	1	Wisconsin		7
Arkansas	1	Iowa		9
Missouri	66	District of Columbia		10
Ohio	222	Nova Scotia		1
Indiana	97	Canada		3
Illinois	56	Africa		1
Kentucky	68	Unknown		11

TRADES AND OCCUPATIONS.

Farmers	596	Firemen	2
Laborers	74	Coppersmith	1
Barbers	34	Machinist	1
Waiters	50	Rope-maker	1
Cooks	27	Fisherman	1
Blacksmiths	21	Tinker	1
Painters	7	Harness-maker	1
Teamsters	27	Caulker	1
Grooms	7	Glass-grinder	1
Hostlers	9	Musician	1
Coachmen	3	Moulder	1
Coopers	5	Confectioner	1
Sailors	20	Tobacco-worker	1
Butchers	8	Clergyman	1
Iron-workers	2	Broom-maker	1
Shoemakers	9	Baker	1
Masons and Plasterers	16	Student	1
Brick-makers	3		
Whitewashers	2	No. who had been slaves	247
Stonecutters	2	No. pure blacks	550
Printers	3	No. mixed blood	430
Boatmen	6	No. who could read	477
Teachers	6	No. who could read and	
Clerks	5	write	319
Porters	5	No. church-members	52
Carpenters	6	No. married	219
Wagon-makers	2	Average age	$23\frac{1}{5}$ years
Millers	2	Average height	$5\frac{7}{12}$ feet [1]
Engineers	3		

Every school has its obstreperous boys, every class at
Harvard has its fast men, every regiment in the service had
its hard characters. The problem to be solved in almost

---

[1] Record of the service of the 55th Regiment of Mass. Vols. Infantry,
110 *et seq.*

every congregation of men is not so much the care of the virtuous many as the discipline of the troublesome few. Colonel Robert Gould Shaw was not a sentimentalist. He imposed the strict discipline of the Second Regiment, from which he came, upon the Fifty-fourth. The men of a slave regiment required, and in the case of the First South Carolina received, treatment very different from that required by mixed regiments like the Fifty-fourth and Fifty-fifth. In a slave regiment the harsher forms of punishment were, or ought to have been, unknown, so that every suggestion of slavery might be avoided This was Colonel T. W. Higginson's enlightened method, — the method of kindness, and it was successful. Colonel Shaw's method was the method of coercion, and it too was successful. The unruly members of the Fifty-fourth and Fifty-fifth were stood on barrels, bucked, gagged and, if need be, shot; in fact, treated as white soldiers were in all well-disciplined regiments. The squads of recruits which arrived at Readville for the Fifty-fifth could hardly at first sight have been called picked men. They were poor and ragged. Upon arrival they were marched to the neighboring pond, disrobed, washed and uniformed. Their old clothes were burnt. The transformation was quite wonderful. The recruit was very much pleased with the uniform. He straightened up, grew inches taller, lifted, not shuffled, his feet, began at once to try, and to try hard, to take the position of the soldier, the facings and other preliminary drill, so that his ambition to carry "one of those muskets" might be gratified. When finally he was entrusted with the responsible duties of a guard, there was nothing quite so magnificent and, let me add, quite so reliable, as the colored volunteer. The effect of camp dis-

cipline on his character was very marked. His officers
were gentlemen who understood the correct orthography
and pronunciation of the word "negro." For the first
time in his life he found himself respected, and entrusted
with duties, for the proper performance of which he would
be held to a strict accountability. Crossing the camp
lines by connivance of the guard was almost unknown.
" Running guard" was an experiment too dangerous to
try. The niceties of guard-mounting and guard-duty, the
absolute steadiness essential to a successful dress-parade,
were all appreciated and faithfully observed. The clean-
liness of the barracks and camp grounds at Readville was
a delight. Not a scrap of loose floating paper or stuff
of any kind was permitted. The muskets, the accoutre-
ments, were kept clean and polished. Every one was
interested, every one did his best. The Sunday morning
inspections discovered a degree of perfection that received
much praise from several regular as well as veteran volunteer officers. It is not extravagant to say that thousands
of strangers who visited the camp were instantly converted
by what they saw. The aptitude of the colored volunteer
to learn the manual of arms, to execute readily the orders
for company and regimental movements, and his apparent
inability to march out of time at once arrested the attention of every officer. His power of imitation was great,
his memory for such movements was good, and his ear for
time or cadence perfect. You may call the imitative
power a sign of inferiority, or what you will. We have
now to do with the negro as a soldier, and as such it may
be accurately said that the average colored soldier adapts
himself more readily to the discipline of a camp, and
acquires what is called the drill, in much less time than

the average white soldier. These characteristics stand out clear and undisputed by those who have had experience in both kinds of regiments. Treated kindly and respectfully, the average colored citizen is the most inoffensive of persons. He prefers to get out of rather than in your way. Innately he is a gentleman. Instinctively he touches his hat when passing. The requirements of military discipline were very favorable for the full development of these traits, so much so that in the matter of etiquette and polite manners one felt that he was in command of a regiment of a thousand men, — each man a possible Lord Chesterfield.

FORT WAGNER.

Fort Wagner was situated on the north end of Morris Island, Charleston Harbor. It was an enclosed work constructed of huge timbers and rafters, covered over with earth and sand, some twenty feet thick. In its bomb-proof shelter a garrison varying from 750 to 1400 effective men withstood with trifling loss the bombardment which lasted almost uninterruptedly night and day for fifty days. The terrible fire of the Federal land batteries and the " Ironsides," eight monitors and five gunboats, seemed sure to tear out the very insides of the fort, but, in fact, simply excited a lively commotion in the sand. It was surrounded with a ditch and provided with a sluice-gate for retaining the high tides. It extended from high-water mark on the east, six hundred and thirty feet, to Vincent's Creek and the impassable marshes on the west. It was armed with eighteen guns of various calibre, of which number, fifteen covered the only approach by land, which was along the beach and was the width of scarcely half a company front in one place. This approach was swept not only by the guns of Wagner, but also by those of Battery Gregg on Cumming's Point, the very northern extremity of the island, and by those of Sumter, and it was enfiladed by several heavily-armed batteries on James and Sullivan Islands.

The first assault, in which the colored troops took no part, was made on the morning of July 11th, 1863. General Gillmore officially reported: " The parapet was gained, but the support recoiled under the fire to which they were exposed, and would not be gotten up." The second and more famous assault was made at twilight on the evening of July 18th, by two brigades,' the one under command of Brigadier-General Strong, the other under Colonel Putnam, and the whole under Brigadier-General Seymour. The First Brigade was designated to storm the fort, the Second to support the First. Our Fifty-fourth Massachusetts led the column. In quick time that devoted column went on to its destiny, heedless of the gaps made in its ranks by the relentless fire of the guns of Wagner, of Gregg, of Sumter, of James and Sullivan Islands. When within two hundred yards of the fort, the fire from the Federal batteries ceased, so that our men might not be destroyed by it. In an instant the rebel garrison swarmed from the bomb-proof to the parapet, and to its artillery was added the compact and destructive fire of fourteen hundred rifles at two hundred yards' range, a storm of solid shot, shells, grape, canister and bullets that annihilated the head of the column and staggered for the moment the regiments that followed. Something must be done, and that quickly, or everything would go down under that appalling fire. Not with the intoxicated cheer of men who rush on to victory, but with the reckless

shout that men give when they lead a forlorn hope, the
two hundred yards were passed, the ditch was crossed, the
parapet was gained, and the State and National colors
planted thereon.

A characteristic of veteran troops is that they cannot
always be made to attempt the seemingly impossible.
Over and over again we read of soldiers tried in many a
campaign, who, though hearing orders, heed them not, but
stand appalled and benumbed. A characteristic of the
white veterans who were engaged in the two assaults on
Wagner was that they "could not be got up," that is to
say in sufficient numbers to push the advantage gained to
complete success. On the second assault fragments of
regiments survived the narrow passage on the beach and
put in an appearance within the fort. Other fragments,
unable to scale the parapet, found shelter by lying down
on the slope of the fort. Colonel John L. Chatfield with
his Sixth Connecticut and fragments of the Fifty-fourth
Massachusetts and other regiments occupied the south-
east bastion. The Thirty-first North Carolina Regiment
(Confederate), which was to have defended that bastion
or salient, demoralized by a new and strange experience,
failed to respond, and remained in the bomb-proof. For
one hour the captured bastion was held against the inces-
sant attacks of the enemy, who now added pikes and
hand grenades to their weapons of defence and assault.
It was a valiant garrison, hard pressed, and was driven,
for a moment, from one side of the work to seek shelter
among the traverses; but when reinforced from Sumter,
at the critical moment, it triumphed.

Colonel Shaw fell dead upon the parapet. Captains
Russell and Simpkins and other brave men fell while

keeping the embrasures free from the enemy's gunners and
sweeping the crest of the parapet with their fire.[1] Lieu-
tenant-Colonel Edward N. Hallowell reached the parapet.
Desperately wounded, he rolled into the ditch, was again
hit, and with great difficulty managed to crawl to our
lines. An unknown number of enlisted men were killed
within the fort. Forty enlisted men, including twenty
wounded, were captured within the fort. The State flag,
tied, unfortunately, to the staff with ribbons, was lost.
The staff itself was brought off. The national colors
planted upon the parapet were upheld and eventually
borne off by Sergeant William H. Carney, a heroic man
whose wounds in both legs, in the breast and the right
arm, attest his devotion to his trust. The regiment went
into action with twenty-two officers and six hundred and
fifty enlisted men. Fourteen officers were killed or
wounded. Two hundred and fifty-five enlisted men were
killed or wounded. Prisoners, not wounded, twenty. Total
casualties, officers and men, two hundred and sixty-nine,
or forty per cent. The character of the wounds attest the
nature of the contest. There were wounds from bayonet
thrusts, sword cuts, pike thrusts and hand grenades; and
there were heads and arms broken and smashed by the
butt-ends of muskets.

As bearing upon the disposition of Colonel Shaw's body
we have the letter of Assistant-Surgeon John T. Luck,
U.S.A., dated at New York, October 21, 1865 : —

To the Editor of the Army and Navy Journal —

Sir, — I was taken prisoner by the rebels the morning
after the assault on Fort Wagner, South Carolina, July 19th,
1863. While being conducted into the fort I saw Colonel
Shaw, of the Fifty-fourth Massachusetts (colored) Regi-

---

[1] Emilio's Fort Wagner, 12.

ment, lying dead upon the ground just outside the parapet.
A stalwart negro had fallen near him. The rebels said the
negro was a color-sergeant. The colonel had been killed
by a rifle-shot through the chest, though he had received
other wounds. Brigadier-General Hagood, commanding the
rebel forces, said to me : "I knew Colonel Shaw before the
war, and then esteemed him. Had he been in command of
white troops I should have given him an honorable burial.
As it is, I shall bury him in the common trench, with the
negroes that fell with him." [1]

General Hagood affirms that he has no recollection of
the conversation as given by Surgeon Luck, and attempts
to show that Colonel Shaw's burial in the trench with his
negroes was without significance. There appears, however, to be no good reason for changing the record. The
manner of Colonel Shaw's burial has been circumstantially
related by two Confederate officers, — Major McDonald,
Fifty-first North Carolina, and Captain H. W. Hendricks, —
both of whom were present at the time. Colonel Shaw's
body was stripped of all his clothing save undershirt and
drawers. This desecration of the dead was done by one
Charles Blake and others. The body was carried within
the fort and there exposed for a time. It was then carried
without the fort and buried in a trench with the negroes.
Colonel Shaw was the only officer buried with the colored
troops [2]

"I know not," said Governor Andrew as he handed the
colors to the Fifty-fourth, "when, in all human history, to
any given thousand men in arms there has been given a
work so proud, so precious, so full of hope and glory, as
the work committed to you."

[1] Harvard Memorial Biographies, 211.
[2] Emilio's History of the Fifty-fourth Regiment, 98 *et seq.*, and 226.

Colonel Shaw was in the twenty-sixth year of his age,—how young it seems now!—and had seen two years of hard service in the Army of the Potomac. His clean-cut face, quick, decided step, and singular charm of manner, full of grace and virtue, bespoke the hero. The immortal charge of his black regiment reads like a page of the Iliad or a story from Plutarch. I have always thought that in the great war with the slave power the figure that stands out in boldest relief is that of Colonel Shaw. There were many others as brave and devoted as he, — the humblest private who sleeps in yonder cemetery or fills an unknown grave in the South is as much entitled to our gratitude, — but to no others was given an equal opportunity. By the earnestness of his convictions, the unselfishness of his character, his championship of an enslaved race, and the manner of his death, all the conditions are given to make Shaw the best historical exponent of the underlying cause, the real meaning of the war. He was the fair type of all that was brave, generous, beautiful, and of all that was best worth fighting for in the war of the slaveholders' Rebellion.

Yes, the colored troops fought well. That is not the most that may be said for men. The courage that is necessary to face death in battle is not of the highest order. The lower the scale of civilization the higher the degree of that kind of courage. It is all very well of course to praise the bravery of these men as soldiers, but with what words may we express our admiration of the dignity, self-respect, self-control, they showed in their conduct as men as well as soldiers in the matter of pay? They were promised the same pay, and, in general, the same treatment, as white soldiers. No one expected the same treatment in the sense of courtesy, but every one believed a

Col. Robert G. Shaw.

great nation would keep faith with its soldiers in the beggarly matter of pay. They were promised thirteen dollars per month. They were insulted with an offer of seven dollars. Massachusetts resented the insult, and attempted to remedy the wrong by offering to make good the difference between the thirteen dollars promised and the seven dollars offered. The State agents, with money in hand, visited the camps on Folly and Morris islands, and pleaded with the men by every argument, by every persuasion they could command. In vain; they were the soldiers of the Union, not of a State. They would receive their pay in full from the United States, or they would not receive it at all. The Nation might break its faith, but they would keep theirs. Every mail brought letters from wives and children asking for money. In some instances their homes were broken up and the almshouse received their families. At times the regiments were driven to the verge of mutiny. In point of fact, the Fifty-fifth did one morning stack arms, not in an angry, tumultuous way, but in a sullen, desperate mood that expressed a wish to be marched out to be shot down rather than longer hear the cries from home and longer endure the galling sense of humiliation and wrong. But better counsels prevailed, and a grand catastrophe was averted by the patriotism and innate good sense of the men, added to the infinite patience, tact, and firmness of the officers. One poor fellow, a sergeant in the Third South Carolina, induced his company to stack arms on the ground that he was " released from duty by the refusal of the Government to fulfil its share of the contract." He was logical, but it was in time of war, and the only thing to be done, was done. He was court-martialled and shot. In the scathing words of Governor

Andrew: "The Government which found no law to pay him except as a nondescript and a contraband, nevertheless found law enough to shoot him as a soldier." Seven times were our regiments mustered for pay. Seven times they refused, and pointed to their honorable scars to plead their manhood and their rights. The men of the Fifty-fifth for sixteen, of the Fifty-fourth for eighteen, months toiled on and fought on without one cent of pay, and at last they won, — won through long suffering and patient endurance; won through a higher and rarer courage than the courage of battle, — a victory that is not inscribed on their flags by the side of Wagner, of James Island, of Olustee, and of Honey Hill, but which none the less fills one of the noblest and brightest pages in the history of their race, as it does one of the most disgraceful in the record of our war.

In January of the year 1781, under conditions far less exasperating, the American army quartered at Morristown mutinied for lack of pay, declared their intention of departing to their homes, and were only restrained from carrying their threat into execution by the personal influence and solicitation of the Commander-in Chief.[1]

The tender of full payment from date of enlistment, when finally made by the United States, was made to those only who would make oath that they were free on or before April 21, 1861. We must thoroughly respect the tender consciences of two or three men who could not in strict conformity with the truth and who did not make this oath, and who therefore never received their pay, but we have no harsh words for the many who were equal to the occasion by swearing to their freedom on April 21st,

---

[1] History of the Bank of North America, 24.

or any other day. Those who were fugitive slaves, and
hence in a legal sense not free at the time specified, had
overcome too many difficulties in their escape from the
South, and in their efforts to avoid the slave-hounds in the
North, to be seriously annoyed by this grotesque proposition
to swear away their back pay by denying their freedom.

Fort Wagner was finally reduced by regular siege operations extending from July 18th to September 7th, 1863.
Five approaches or parallels were run across the island
from the right to the marshes on the left; the fifth and
last parallel was within two hundred and forty yards of
the fort. In its construction the remains of Federal soldiers who had been buried by the rebels after the assaults
were excavated. The ground was thick with torpedoes,
which were removed, not without some distressing casualties. Their presence explained the inactivity of the garrison, which hitherto had been a mystery. This reliance upon
torpedoes instead of upon constant sorties to harass the
fatigue parties and to delay or destroy their works is noted
by Gillmore and others as the capital defect in the defence
of Wagner A further trench, which may be called a
branch of the fifth parallel, permitted an approach within
one hundred yards. Indeed, on the night preceding the
evacuation, the sappers pushed on by the south face, leav-
ing it at their left, and removing a sort of palisade made
up of projecting pikes and sharp-pointed stakes " firmly
planted in the counterscarp of the ditch." By means of
calcium lights the fort was kept well illuminated, and our
own men all the more enshrouded in darkness. The work
was done under constant fire and almost altogether at
night. Finally, on the morning of September 7th, when
General Gillmore was again prepared to assault, both

Wagner and Gregg were evacuated with the trifling loss to the rebels of two boats containing nineteen sailors and twenty-seven soldiers of the rear guard. In the somewhat contemptuous language of the Confederate Major Robert C. Gilchrist, "Seven hundred and forty men were driven out of a sandhill by eleven thousand five hundred."

The following official inquiries were made of the engineers who directed the operations of working parties of both white and black troops during the siege of Wagner:

1. Courage, as indicated by their behavior under fire.

2. Skill and appreciation of their duties, referring to the quality of the work performed.

3. Industry and perseverance with reference to the quantity of the work performed.

4. If a certain work were to be accomplished in the least possible time, $i.\,e.$, when enthusiasm and direct personal interest are necessary to attain the end, would whites or blacks answer best?

5. What is the difference, considering the above points, between colored troops recruited from the free States, and those from the slave States?

Six replies to these inquiries were received from engineer officers who had been engaged in the siege; the substance of them is embraced in the following summary : —

1. To the first question, all answer that the black is more timorous than the white, but is in a corresponding degree more docile and obedient, — hence more completely under the control of his commander, and much more influenced by his example.

2. All agree that the black is less skilful than the white soldier, but still enough so for most kinds of siege work.

3. The statements unanimously agree that the black will do a greater amount of work than the white soldier, because he labors more constantly.

4. The whites are decidedly superior in enthusiasm. The blacks cannot be easily hurried in their work, no matter what the emergency.

5. All agree that the colored troops recruited from the free States are superior to those recruited from slave States.

The average percentage of sick among the negro troops during the siege was 13.9, while that of the white infantry was 20.1 per cent.

The foregoing summary is taken from the appendix to Gillmore's Report, where also two of the replies are given in full, and are supposed to be a fair sample of the others. One of the engineers says: " I will say, in my opinion their courage is rather of the passive than the active kind. They will stay, endure, resist and follow; but they have not the restless, aggressive spirit. I do not believe they will desert their officers in trying moments in so great numbers as the whites; they have not the will, audacity or fertility of excuse of the straggling white, and at the same time they have not the heroic nervous energy or vivid perception of the white, who stands firm or presses forward. I do not remember a single instance, in my labors in the trenches, where the black man has skulked away from his duty, and I know that instances of that kind have occurred among the whites; still, I think that the superior energy and intelligence of those remaining, considering that the whites were the lesser number by the greater desertion, would more than compensate." The other reply reads, in answer to the first inquiry : " I have found that black troops manifest more timidity under

fire than white troops ; but they are, at the same time,
more obedient to orders and more under the control
of their officers, in dangerous situations, than white
soldiers."

The evidence of the engineers was more favorable than
was expected by those who knew them. With the excep-
tion of what they style " superior intelligence " and " enthusiasm," their replies quite make up the beau ideal of a
soldier. To stay, to endure, to resist, to follow, to work
patiently, doggedly, to obey orders, never to skulk, or to
desert their officers in trying moments, — what more do
you expect, what more do you find in the mass of men
who go to make up an army ?   " Superior intelligence "
they had not, — that is an essential for an officer ; average
intelligence may be, " superior intelligence " is not, needed
in the soldier.   The engineers themselves did not want it ;
they did not even want " nervous energy " and " enthusiasm " in the trenches.   The simple fact is, the engineers
clamored for details of black troops, and were always dis-
appointed and provoked when they could not get them.
The engineers were good fellows, most of them.   They
were competent to pass judgment upon the working parties in the trenches, but they did not know how to write it
out.   In their willingness to try to say the fair and the
correct word, they admit more in their comparisons with
the whites than I should care to claim.   Their conclusion
seems to be a jumble ; namely, that although the blacks
did the greater part of the work, did it more faithfully
than the whites, stuck to their officers in trying emer-
gencies more devotedly than did the whites ; that although
they preferred the blacks in the trenches ; yet, after all,
some how or other, they don't exactly know why, yet

they do prefer whites! In the matter of "enthusiasm" the engineers are altogether at fault. In five minutes you can excite a regiment of blacks into a pitch of enthusiasm that will carry everything before it, provided you yourself are sincere; provided you respect and trust them and they respect and trust you; provided always you know how to spell and to pronounce the word "negro," — that sure test and gauge of refinement in an American.

The alleged timidity, want of enthusiasm, heroic nervous energy, and all that sort of thing, is not, for the engineers, very happily illustrated by the next action in which the Fifty-fifth Massachusetts took part. In an effort to surprise Battery Lamar on James Island, the Federal column was itself surprised by a section of artillery posted in an old field-work, and supported, though not heavily, by both cavalry and infantry. One white regiment, a good one too, that has the names of twenty battles inscribed upon its flags, was driven in the utmost confusion to the rear. One colored regiment, armed with nearly worthless old Austrian rifles, soon after condemned, did but little better. The Fifty-fifth went right on in perfect order, charged the battery, captured two twelve-pounder Napoleon guns, turned the guns upon the flying enemy, and brought them off in triumph with a loss of two officers wounded and twenty-six enlisted men killed or wounded. It may be well at this point to pay brief attention to the oft-repeated question, " Did the colored fight as well as the white troops?" by calling the attention of the inquirer to the obvious fact that these captured guns were defended, under favorable conditions, by white troops.

OLUSTEE.

In the disastrous affair of Olustee, Florida, February 20th, 1864, the redeeming feature appears to have been the conspicuous gallantry of the Fifty-fourth Massachusetts. That regiment was hurried into action at the very crisis of affairs. It checked the onward sweep of a victorious enemy, and covered the retreat towards Jacksonville in a thoroughly creditable manner, as I am told, under the immediate direction of Colonel Edward N. Hallowell. In this battle the Eighth U. S. Colored Infantry lost three hundred and ten dead, wounded and missing, — the missing mostly dead or wounded left on the field, — one of the severest regimental losses during the war.

HONEY HILL, S. .C., November 30th, 1864.

This assault, in its main features, was a repetition of Wagner. The only approach attempted to the rebel batteries and intrenchments was the narrow cutting through which the road crossed the swamp. Through this defile five companies of the Fifty-fifth Massachusetts were ordered to storm the enemy's works. The order is not free from the charge of down-right recklessness. Against the concentrated fire of artillery and musketry at one hundred yards' range the five companies charged in vain, were rallied twice and then withdrawn with a loss of twenty-nine killed and one hundred and fifteen wounded, or one half the officers and one third of the enlisted men engaged. A useless slaughter, not compensated for by some brilliant fighting both before and after the charge.

In passing, I desire in affectionate remembrance to simply give the names of Captain William Dwight Crane

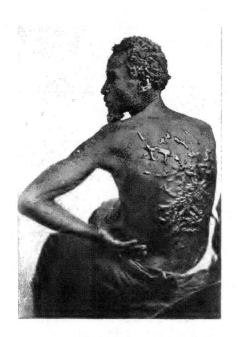

A LACERATED SLAVE.

FROM BATON ROUGE, LA.

and Lieutenant Winthrop Perkins Boynton, who were chums in Harvard College, officers in the same company, devoted friends, who seemed always to move, to think and to act in beautiful accord, and who here fell together in a common death.

Besides these, the more important actions, there were many minor affairs, not large enough to be dignified by the name of battles, but entirely sufficient to test the mettle of the men as soldiers. In these, our Massachusetts regiments appear to have been uniformly successful. There were reconnoissances and raids, rifle pits were charged and captured, prisoners were taken, and the resources of the enemy removed or destroyed. There is not time, nor is it necessary, to more than mention the conspicuous service rendered by the colored troops in the other military departments.

PORT HUDSON.

At Port Hudson and at Milliken's Bend, Louisiana, the official reports commend the colored troops for steadiness in maintaining positions and for heroism in charging the batteries of the enemy.

In a paper read before the Military Historical Society of Massachusetts, by General John C. Palfrey, the conduct of the black regiments at Port Hudson, June 27, 1863, is recorded in these forceful words : " Between the attacks of Weitzel and Augur an assault was ordered from our extreme right by the black regiments as a diversion. Their ground was very difficult and disadvantageous, and the garrison received them with special temper and exasperation. But they fought without panic, and suffered severely before falling back in good order. Their conduct and its indication of character and manliness made a profound impression on the army, and later through the country. The day should be one of the famous dates in the progress of their race."

PETERSBURG.

At the first attempt on Petersburg, Virginia, in June, 1864, Hinks' Division of the 18th Corps, under fire for the first time, carried the line of works in its front, and captured in succession seven pieces of artillery with great spirit and dash. This decided success of the colored troops gave to General Smith an opportunity to seize Petersburg, advantage of which, however, was not taken, whether through a misinterpretation of General Grant's orders, or because the city was believed to be untenable, is a matter of considerable debate.

CHAFFIN'S FARM AND FORT GILMER.

Paine's Division of the 18th Corps and Birney's Colored Division of the 10th Corps were conspicuously engaged at Chaffin's Farm, in the assault on Fort Gilmer and the intrenchments at New Market Heights. At Fort Gilmer they scaled the parapet by climbing upon each other's backs. A distinguished rebel general wrote at the time: "Fort Gilmer proved the other day that they would fight."

THE CRATER.

At the battle of the Crater, at Petersburg, July 30th, 1864, the colored troops were ordered in after the assault was a bloody failure. They failed to retrieve the disaster, but were in no way responsible for it. Their casualties in Ferrero's Division were 1327 killed, wounded and

Col. Edward N. Hallowell.
BREVET BRIG. GEN. U. S. V.

missing. The white soldiers in the Crater were permitted to surrender; many of the blacks were given no quarter.

NASHVILLE.

In the victory at Nashville, December 16th, 1864, the heaviest loss in any regiment occurred in the 13th U. S. Colored Infantry,— 55 killed and 106 wounded : total 221. General George H. Thomas, the hero of that battle, a Virginian and at one time a slaveholder, when riding over the field, saw the dead colored troops commingled with the bodies of the white soldiers, and said, " This proves the manhood of the negro." [1]

Fox enumerates 52 battles and actions in which colored troops were prominently engaged, and from the same authority it appears that before the war closed there were 145 regiments of infantry, 7 of cavalry, 12 of heavy artillery, 1 of light artillery, and 1 of engineers : total 166. Of these, about 60 were brought into action on the battlefield, the others having been assigned to post or garrison duty. Fox makes the following judicial remark : " Of the regiments brought into action, only a few were engaged in more than one battle; the war was half over, and so the total of killed does not appear as great as it otherwise would have done. The total number killed or mortally wounded was 143 officers and 2751 men." [2] The actual fighting done by the colored troops was not, under the conditions stated, inconsiderable. The indirect benefit to our armies was incalculable. When General Grant gathered together his forces to make the supreme effort that

[1] Van Horn's Life of Thomas, 347.
[2] Fox's Regimental Losses, 56.

culminated in the capitulation of General Lee, he added
to his Army of the Potomac the white veterans that held
the forts, the cities and the islands of the Atlantic Coast,
as well as some of the more interior parts of the mainland.
The vacated points must be held against the enemy by
some one. They were so held by the colored troops. I
am not able to state accurately the number of reinforce-
ments thus contributed to the Army of the Potomac.
Certainly the entire 10th Army Corps was relieved and
sent to Virginia. It is probably safe to say that 40,000
men is not an over-estimate. When we remember that
General Grant lost 60,000 men in 60 days, a number equal
to General Lee's effective army at that time, it well be-
comes a question worthy the serious attention of the
historian what might have been the fate of Grant's Army
in the Wilderness had there been 40,000 fewer veterans
than there were.

It remains to be recited that in the last desperate days
of the expiring Rebellion the Confederate Congress passed
a bill which provided that not more than twenty-five per
cent of the male slaves between the ages of eighteen and
forty-five should be called out. It is worthy of note that
General Lee gave his unqualified advocacy of the proposed
measure. Unfortunately the passage of the act had been
so long delayed that the Confederacy collapsed before
results were obtained. I wish it had been otherwise. I
have no hesitation in saying that the slave regiments
would have deserted *en masse* to the Yankees, and that
the supposition that they would have fought for the Confederacy is hugely and grotesquely preposterous.

In conclusion, let us never forget the debt we owe to
the colored soldiers. Let us always be willing to give

them whatever credit is their due. We called upon them in the day of our trial, when volunteering had ceased, when the draft was a partial failure and the bounty system a senseless extravagance. They were ineligible for promotion, they were not to be treated as prisoners of war. Nothing was definite except that they could be shot and hanged as soldiers. Fortunate indeed is it for us, as well as for them, that they were equal to the crisis; that the grand historic moment which comes to a race only once in many centuries came to them, and that they recognized it. They saw that the day of their redemption had arrived. They escaped through the rebel lines of the South; they came from all over the North; and, when the war closed, the names of one hundred and eighty-six thousand men of African descent were on the rolls.

CPSIA information can be obtained
at www.ICGtesting.com
Printed in the USA
BVHW040422110720
583375BV00008B/305